Scrumpers

by

Roy T. Morgans

*For Evelyn*

First published in 2020

ISBN 978-1-8380150-0-8

A catalogue record for this book is available
from the British Library

Printed and bound by
Abbey Bookbinding & Print, Cardiff, Wales

## Acknowledgements

This collection would not have come to fruition without the
encouragement, patience and expertise of Kath and Kristian; Ally and
Darrel; Aberdare Poetry Society; The Sounding Bowl Crickhowell,
Mike Jenkins and Robert King.

With special thanks to Maureen.

### Warren Williams, the artist
Warren grew up on a diet of wrestling, horror, sci- fi and reading
2000AD comics against the backdrop of the South Wales valleys. He
now lives in South London illustrating and running an architectural
practice with his wife.

# Contents

# I. Wild Bunch

# Hideaway

This is a boys' den
concealed in a June jungle
that I have stumbled
on: a green hideaway
deep in a secrecy of trees
exclusive to feral boys –
not a place for men.

Still, I enter, stand,
and peer all about, despite
the big  KEEP OUT
in purple paint
upon a propped zinc sheet,
        signed: *Miv, Slug,*
*Spike, Zonka.*

But, I linger
under a lush canopy
of hazel-leaf and ash
where boys' boots have panned
to clay the sorrel stems
and blades of grass
and made a clear patch.

A log and two flat stones
are seats set round a hearth
that holds wood-ash of many fires.
And for roasting spuds
four hazel sticks, black-tipped...
This is a hearth for wild boys
where I don't belong. And yet –

to satisfy some boyish need
I choose a charcoal stub
and beside their names upon
the zinc, I add my own, knowing
that it won't be seen.
Soon, dark clouds will send the rain
to wipe away that I have been...

## Savages

We were eight, all told,
and we lived apart
in a tight neighbourhood of terraced rows –
though together,
we marauded the wood.

Birds weren't safe.

We were raiders and wreckers
who knew all of *Tawny's* hidden holes and hollows,
could shin to the high tenement where *Raven* lay
on her bleak, stick bed.
Not even *Maggie's* Ali Baba basket –
her barbed fortress –
lay beyond our upward reach.

Trees weren't safe.

We dishonoured *Hazel* for staff and spear;
de-flowered *May*. Laid *Birch*
lower than a ship's mast in a force ten.
We'd hug the long legs of *Ash,*
ape up her, by nails and heaves
to tattoo our names on her trunk.
We'd strip *Willow* for whippings;
chop the soft fingers of *Sallow* for whistles.

We weren't safe.

always high in *Ivy*
or *Holly*, raw-kneed and shin-raked;
but to engage *Alder* – long-bodied and proud
whose elegant wide-spreading limbs
were as brittle as balsa –
was the stiffest test of our nerve.
Lots drawn, short-straw would swing out
hand-over-hand on a high limb till the **crack**
and the cheered down-crash
of boy and branch.

Then the next up –

but to a higher limb –
and then the next boy, even higher, and the next, and
all the way up to long-straw who had the
farthest to fall.
There were sprains, and cuts that bled,
there were grazes and bruises
to head and rib and leg…

and for weeks, *Alder* wept her rusty blood.

## Scrumpers

Tree high in the humid dark we scrumped
forbidden fruit, fingered through night-leaves
for fat, green globes, stretched for big ones that weighed
the tips low. A tweak and they snapped clean, came plump
and cool into the cupped hand – each one precious,
every one ours. We stripped the top limbs first,
picked towards ground, slid fruit after fruit
down the necks of our ragged jerseys, to be trapped
at the waist by tight string tourniquets.
Under a faint rustling of leaves we thieved
in the still night, (gagging each nervous cuss
and giggle as bent boughs lifted, unburdened, bare)
thumbs and fingers sticky with stem-sap,
intoxicated by the apple-perfumed air.

We slumped to ground, heavy with apples, cloaked
ourselves in shadow under the orchard wall;
went down on our bare knees in the dark grass –
untying string, we loosed the fragrant haul,
heaped emerald plunder between us.
The fruit you chose appeared too big for the grasp
of your small hands; you bit through skin, crisp flesh
thirsty for juices, but cringed and almost choked
at the bitter taste. Then the bright flick
that freeze-framed us in lurid light – loud thunder
and the first fat drops heavy as lead-grain
splattering leaves – the Big Man's roar of anger –
and we were running, you ahead, your hip-
length hair glistening in the quickening rain…

## Of Monkeys, Kings and Conquerors

They came for conkers
through the cool of morning;
went quiet by the Big House and passed
to the ancient wood beside the Caiach brook:

a band of Trelewis lads and
one wild Bedlinog boy.
From the stream-side cottages
came two little sisters for a share
of chestnut treasure.

They came for conkers –
and all were would-be-conquerors:
Tudor and Paul, Gwyn, Dai and Lewis –
now, sixty odd years on – of the many,
these the only names recalled.

And that wild Bedlinog boy –
being of arboreal bent – went squirreling aloft;
and as he rose, from below he overheard
a grounded boy's philosophy:
*Don't look up*
*a horse-chestnut*
*when monkey shakes the tree.*

All that morning
and through the blue of noon
to the autumn sun's declining,
for that wild boy time was absent – was somewhere
else with clocks, clock-makers, and kings.

For him, there was only leaf-storm, only the bounce and
scatter, the tap and pattering of conker-
fall through the thrash and crash of branches;
and as if in answer, from
far below, rose hoots of joy, triumphant shouts
and laughter from the mouths of
unseen boys and girls.

Just once, fleetingly, he sensed
he was not alone in the dizzying air,
perhaps there was a face – pale and thin –
amidst the knots and knarls, high
under the shadowing crown of a near tree…
but the thought went.

For what meagre grasp,
if at all, does a young monkey have
of time and history and kings.
Perhaps, across a distance, there *was*
some other.

Maybe, fugitive and veiled
by autumn's ochre and gold confetti fall, imperious eyes
somewhat amused, watched a silly monkey
shake a tree…


*In august 1645 the ill fated King Charles1. visited Llancaiach Manor
at Nelson. His son, Charles 2., to avoid Cromwell's forces, concealed
himself in the 'Royal Oak' in Worcester. Among Trelewis kids a rumour
circulated that to dodge Roundheads, some king hid in a tree in Trelewis.*

# Nantwen Pit

When we played hide-and-seek or tag
through the tumbled brick and mortar
ruin of the mine, we shunned the tower
that loomed high above the slag:

a brick stack more secure than a jail,
a blank-walled, ochre coloured drum
that afforded hardly any fun,
for its sheer sides we could not scale.

The Bowen brothers started it –
used a bent spike and stolen hammer
to probe and hook-out the good mortar
that retained a big foundation brick.

We larked, while the brothers persevered;
but, on the fourth day as the first block
was heaved and levered from its slot
we loungers gathered round and cheered.

But there was nothing: nothing there
except a solid inner wall.
Though now hooked, each boy in turn fell-
to – every one a great explorer.

And though it rained, we laboured on
until four further bricks were won
and we were almost through. In moonlight, wet and bruised, we ghosted home.

Next day, with girls in tow, we hiked
back. There, mad Dai dared the hard-
won slot, dragged out the final slab
and opened up a hole on night.

Little Mostyn knelt, moled
inside, and yelled back: U*p high*
*there's a bright-blue disc of sky.*
*Below, a bloody big black hole.*

Into the shaft we tumbled slag –
counted heartbeats to the plash,
the fearful far-off booms, the up-rush
of stinking air that made us gag.

We lugged two dram-rails, spanned them clear
across the shaft to a thin ledge
on its far wall: bearers for a bridge,
narrow as a gravedigger's bier.

As Dai inched out across the deep –
we fed him bits of plank and mesh
for decking. To feather our nest
the girls pulled ferns and meadowsweet.

Often we'd roost on those dark rafters
legs dangling and hip to hip;
the boys telling jokes, the girls in fits,
the pit echoing back our laughter.

Summer's end, Dai and Bryn went back
to find the tower gone, the mine sealed
by a big steel plate and a sign
that read: KEEP OUT. So that was that.

Although now, sixty-years-on,
sometimes I wake in a cold sweat
from a dream of falling to dark depths
with white flowers – and
all the boys and girls, are gone…

    *As kids we played among the surface ruins of Nantwen pit.*

## The Blue Tit

In the garden
I held my breath.
From nowhere, in blurs of blue and yellow
the little acrobats came.
Shy at first, they stayed high
on bean-sticks, swung from the tips
of raspberry-canes.
One, bolder than the rest
dropped to the taut string, telegraphed
his tiny weight to my tensed fingers.
His head, blue capped, twitched
all about, but always
back to the bait – the spread
of bread beneath the propped coal-riddle. Then
he bounced in – my tug
dropped the riddle – wire-mesh
between bird and sky.
I held him. Felt the fast tick of his heart
on my palms, marvelled at the quick black eye
in the white-masked face – and
winced at the beak's pinch
on my thumb's webbed flesh. I ran
to the house
the feathered heat in my fist.

In the parlour,
wrapped in a cage of fingers
I raised the feathered bud for Uncle Jack to see.
Blue eyes wide, his face clouded as
he reached gently for the bird;
the exchange was clumsy, fatal
for we didn't see the watcher
tensed upon the hearth.
In a freedom bid, out
through parting finger-bars of four cupped hands
the blue tit flittered – up
to the window's high brightness – his rising arc cut
at height by window net
and the straight-line-lightning-flash
of the grey cat's strike. Then
the fast dead-fall from rail
to floor as the clawed-net tore.
And Puss, with blue tit safe
in her mouth – flashed from the parlour.

In the kitchen,
Granny – having shushed all my crying
into her pinny – gave me milk, sat me
on the wooden, three-legged stool.
Emptied of tears – but still burdened –
I sipped my drink, saw my accomplice slip silently
in, watched her come, tail high,
a yellow feather in her whiskers.
With upturned face
she fixed me with her blank, unblinking stare.
That's when I knew
I bore all the guilt.  Then she, coaxing –
stroking her silky length against my bare legs – miaowed
to me to share my milk.

## A Lion's Confession

This just to say

I have eaten
little Albert who
you were probably
looking for
around the zoo

Forgive me
he was so tender
and so
savoury

(With thanks to Marriot Edgar
and William Carlos Williams)

# II. From Earth and Air

## Ants

At first only one:
a scout? – for certain, and soon
you'll be overrun

when a thousand spill
from behind the cooker on
a lovely April

day when you're half way
through spring clean. Ah, look there, in
single-file array

the six legged brigade –
a fast black thread advancing
on a sugar raid,

heading for your cup
of cooling sweet Glengettie
and that red ketchup

blob on your bacon
butty plate on the kitchen
island top. Hold on

there's another lot
thick clotting round the lip of
the marmalade pot.

You're under attack
and feeling quite overwhelmed,
you begin to whack

with the tea towel.
Stop. Stop right there. What about
your frank avowal

that you really love
all bugs – so drop the towel
and that oven-glove;

show restraint, fall back,
dig in, yield the sugar bowl,
watch them lap and snack

in your sweet cuppa.
Consider a fresh brew and
keep a stiff upper –

and though a no-brainer
you'll have some control if you
own a tea strainer.

# Battleground

This ash tree hedgerow
robs the soil. Flowers wilt
away, will not grow

in the deep shade cast.
Beheading the ash leaders
is a thankless task

for each rooted stump
sprouts a thicket of new shoots –
a strong defiant clump.

Countless times I've cut
the leaders low with bow-saw,
but in greater glut

they rise tall again
and lay a deeper shadow.
I curse them. But then,

these old trees laid claim
to this ground an age ago –
long before I came

with saw and axe to
oust them. Last year's offensive
failed, they rise anew

like a green hydra.
Soon I'll chop and grub again
with shovel and bar

in a sap-blood-mix
as I dream of a fence of
war-free wattle sticks.

# Daws

April, and they're back,
announcing their arrival
with loud Kya! and Chak!

and the sticks they leave
in my yard – the guano spats
the car roof receives.

And this dark duo –
straight from Poe – are so alike
that it's hard to know

the cock from the hen,
till she settles on sticks, and
again and again

he collects a spread
of beetles and slugs to tempt her
with while she's abed.

Then it's to and fro
by both to glut the loud young
with groceries, though

by the end of May
they're gone – leaving an eerie
silence through the day.

They're not troublesome
to me. In spring I'd miss them
if they didn't come –

those dark squatters,
that umbrella-black pair
of chimney-potters.

# Eight Ways of Looking at Jackdaws

Spring. It's Daw plus mate
under the slate; a fall of soot,
twigs in the grate.

A clue is the caw –
light blue eye and the grey head
of the coal-black Daw.

*Jack? Or is it Jane?*
They look the same – could be twins –
the squaw and her swain.

The white owl squats in the belfry.
  The briar's the house of the wren.
    Rooks have a high tree,
      the eagle his eyrie
        but Daws live in the homes of men.

High in the stack
on her nest of stick,
for broody Jane Daw
the weather is bitter.
      Down at the hearth
      a match is struck,
      and in no time at all
      the weather gets better.

Foolish magpies taunt
the cat that pretends to sleep,
but the cautious Daws
      a sensible      distance keep.

Daws that twist and
        tumble    in the sky,    are
not at play –
                they're just shooing the buzzard away…

Before they rest, the starlings dance,
  keep perfect step in footless air,
                        but Daws that
            gather
            together
      to roost    give raucous shouts    and
are like bits of    burnt paper    that go
            tumbling
        all about    and
                    everywhere

## O Low, Last Sun

O low, last sun of Autumn
you have come to my door,
warm and slow are your steps
on the flags of my yard –
and though faint – you are
welcome, uncovering as
you go a worm and a crust
of bread that brings a bird:
a bold jackdaw that hops for
the worm, and doesn't see
the grey cat concealed
in shadow under the hedge –
the she-cat that has ceased
lapping milk from her cup
and is aware of the bird
poised above the worm:
the cold-eyed cat that stares, un-
sheaths her claws and stiffens...

        O low, last sun
of Autumn, today, see no
snapped feather, or red claw,
no blood-wet whisker. Let
the hungry daw settle for
the crumb of bread, the cat
be content to lick the last
of the cream from her cup.
O low, last sun of Autumn
show me a day free of grief,
and let the innocent worm
return to its dark banquet
under the earth...

## The Amazing Adventurer

I first caught sight of him
crossing the deep chasm of
Pwll-y-rhydd; he was

speeding westward
with no deviation or change of
pace, spurning the easy

north/south Sarn Helen –
that ancient avenue of the
Romans – and scooted on

to the impenetrable
centre of the Maes y Gawen
fir forest, there, pausing

just for an instant, before
an abrupt about-
turn, and an almost exact

retracing of his steps
back towards the east – this
considerable distance

covered in a matter of
moments. With my eyeglass
and from my lofty

position above the panorama,
I got the impression he was
compact and oval

in shape, though I found it
impossible to ascertain how
many legs he had

for in the event
he never stayed still long
enough to allow a

detailed observation.
Back east he pressed, fording
the dry bed of the Nedd Fechan

north of Berthlwyd Farm,
whose walls and hedges
(guarding private land) proved no

obstacle to his headlong
progress. All public footpaths
he ignored on a steep north-

east trending climb, up to
the rocky summit of
Carnau Gwynion where he

executed a sharp turn to
the south, onto the high
platform of the

Pillow Mounds, and there
for some seconds, he
indulged in a confusing

sequence of manoeuvres
consisting of spins and stops,
swings and starts, much like

a fairground dodgem – until
all of a sudden he ascended
in an astonishing

jump: a huge leap eastward
over the small hamlet of
Ystradfellte; over all

the houses; the church
tower; the New Inn; and
post office; and

vanished beyond the
edge. What he was, and
the purpose of his journey,

remain a mystery. And
what he found of interest on
the surface of that perfectly

flat, white land – the
Ordnance Map spread
out across my lap –

is beyond my understanding.

## Autumn's Here

Autumn's in the privet hedge
but you wouldn't know it –
in every leaf from toe to head
but it doesn't show it.

The chill has killed the bumblebee;
the fall has climbed the apple tree,
the wind has blown the pippins free –
pigs ate them all, left none for me.

Autumn's settled on the lawn
stopped the grasses growing,
left a patch where ink-caps spawn –
at least there's no more mowing.

Garden gnome seems quite unfazed
at the frost on his face and beard,
he grins at me through a frosty glaze
wicked eyed and pointy eared.

Autumn wind has tugged the leaves
stripped bare the ash tree's crown –
next blow will pluck the ripened keys
and send them twirling down.

Yellow are the banners of hazel
the flare of their glory so brief;
red flame the flags of the maple –
their going a kind of grief…

## The Himalayans

It's not till mid June when they hoist
colours above green camouflage
that you become aware of them –

and it strikes you for the first time
that they're taking over our Cymru,
crowding both banks of the Cynon,

thronging track-sides in rank and file
all along from Cwmbach to Tynte
and down to Ponty: a pink flagged

invasion force. Some stir, or just
nod as you hurry through, otherwise
their only interest appears

to be the annexation of land,
an army of occupation,
ousting locals and defending

taken ground against all-comers.
But come the cold they furl colours –
when desultory popping might

be heard as they hurl barrages
of grenades – and disappear.
They leave a ravaged ground, a tip:

rusting iron, beer cans, bottles,
the odd boot. Next year they'll rise
in overwhelming numbers.
                              Count on it.

## Two Courses

I dozed on my veranda, gowned
in softest down and tawny quills,
when all at once an awful sound:
weak tragic tweets and little trills
that rose to me from close below –
a robin sobbing in the snow.

Beside the redbreast stiffly lay
his sweet brown hen – once loving mate
feathers fluffed and cold as clay.
Though unsettled at their sorry state
I got tired of the noise, and thought:
what gain to me their plight had brought.

So, descending silent as a sigh
to a white cloth – without a waiter –
I froze the redbreast with my eye.
No bill to pay, and much, much later
I gulped, and hawked-up from my gills
two red pellets of bones and quills.

## Snail

October, and it seemed she had found
her wintering place: my bathroom window,
mucused herself to the leaf pattern
on the outside of the pane –
so that every time I flossed
her foot was in my face.

She was no voyeur: her stalked eyes
always stayed tucked away
in her clockwise house; though every morning
when I brushed my teeth, washed, maybe shaved –
no matter what the weather: frost, wind, or rain –
she was there, presenting, revealing
her sole to me.

The days of her stay mounted,
as did my anticipation of her presence there,
my growing fondness for
the small innocent intimacy.
In the window's outer reveal it appeared
she had found an ideal haven, sheltered as it was
between the green fall of the living ivy
and the leaf embossed glass.

Morning of the thirteenth day –
tap turned, awaiting the warm – I raised
my roller-blind and found she'd gone.
I have to admit a feeling akin to grief
washed in. Had she died – mugged by a crow?
Gone on a browse for breakfast?
No way to know. Perhaps tiring of me,
she'd simply trailed away.

That night, in rain and darkness, I sprinted
from car to rear yard; and as my foot descended on
the door threshold, from under the sole of my shoe
came a sickening sound – sort of crunched cornflakes
and squelched jelly. And out of my conflicted feelings
at the spatter – the surprise coming together –
up popped a thought: *How much
one's size matters.*

# III. Trees and Stones

## The Crowding Forest

The fir trees gather darkness as they crowd
the wood, for in their heaving up for height,
their shouldering and longing for the light –
they spread a shade that deepens to a shroud.
Though crowded close, these living palisades
rise clean, as sheer as schooner masts they climb
covening the resin-scented high arcades
where only a quiet creaking speaks of time.
A savage place: gloom-kingdom for the tall
and able that reach high and overbear
the slow and weak, for there are those that loll
aslant and stiff that have lost the race for sky
and are declining into darkness where
the seeded children of the selfish lie.

## Herald

Here, under faint green light, where
  aged grey verticals soar
out of sight, where low green-bearded boughs bar
  all travellers – is sanctum.
No boot has ever disturbed the amber and ochre
  underlay of deep pine needles.
Overhead in the dim canopy, tweet of finch
  and twitter of siskin hardly break
  into the slow, heavy, silence.

  But now, from the forest edge an axe
speaks: Chack!... Chack!...     The songs of finches cease
                      in a stiffening silence...
A hacking cough of echoes
                  *Chack!... Chack!...*
                  from a distant hill –
  soon
        the cr-eak-ing of a stiff hinge and a crac-k-l-ing – Crash!
  ...loud clap of a wood pigeon bailing-out
of a standing hush –
                  the whole wood – listening...

# Huggasaurs

Huggasaurs are large, come in flashy colours
like bright yellow, or striped orange and black,
go lumbering along with growl, squeak and clack
and armed with teeth and claws, make lethal lovers.
Assertive, they get in close, give no quarter
embracing the chosen in a fierce grip –
insatiable killers intent on slaughter
they slice and chop, decapitate and strip.
Huggasaurs are brash and thoughtless, seem bent
on chaos, blinkered to the death they spread,
leave grey deltas of heaped entanglement
a desolation of limb, stump and head,
a chewed up resinous, diesel smelling mess –
they create deserts in our wilderness.

*Huggasaur is one type of*
*tree harvesting machine*

## The Briar Garden

Gloved, and armed with secateurs and saw
I mounted the steep steps from the
shadowed yard. But at the top I was stopped
by an eight foot wall of briars bathed in
late September sunlight...

Green leaders laden with juicy fruit curved up
arching over my head. Where to begin?
I felt discouraged.  But then a sly leader
spiked my wrist – drew blood – and
I was hooked...

Autumn: bramble stems thick as sweeping brush
handles were chopped and sawn, and as
gloves, jeans and shoes turned purple, I felt guilt
at the waste: robbing magpie, maggot and blackbird
of so much fruit...

Winter: with a rake I thrashed the green barbed wire
down; then the drawn-out drudgery of loading
vicious coils into Hippo bags to be
carted away...

February: I stood on a steep slope of bare earth
studded with green and biscuit-coloured blunt thumbs –
the nubs of the guillotined...

But I'm not fooled: in a kind of treachery, April's push
will send again toothed leaves and shoots. So I pray that
poison can kill the devil at root...

Soap and water have washed away each purple bruise.
Cuts and scratches on ankle and hand have cooled.
Yet even now, weeks later, I wince at the surprise
needles in sock or shoe...

## Mossy

I bought a little old house,
freehold, signed the dotted line;
moved in where every stone was mine
including the very big one aside the back
door. And being the new kid on the block,
I couldn't assent to an oversize obstructive rock.
And so, naming her Mossy ('cause she had a greeny
mop) I told her straight she had to go – being just a
nuisance boulder. So I picked around her, pinched her
with my crowbar – attempted to roll her – and almost
cussed her when I bruised my shoulder. Exhausted
I clung to her, cajoled her saying: *you have a smooth
curved back, sleek sides and a proud bosom; you have
lovely locks on top, and though I have endeavoured hard, sad
to say, I have never viewed your bottom.* In my weak state
I could have sworn that she replied: *I am Mossy – not a
rock-for-rolling:* which brought to mind a sad Greek up and
down a mountain – such a fuss – and anyway by then
I'd had enough. And so, I got planning permission
for a new rear lean-to extension to hold her; and
though it's always down to me to maintain
her hair in good condition, ours is the only
house in the street that features a
solid, green haired, en suite boulder.

## Leavings

For weeks
I kept the windows shut,
curtains closed, and fled away –
driven to my farthest corner to sulk
and cringe there at the din:
clap of plank, the metal clank,
the tubular ring of scaffolding:
my neighbours had the builders in...

All day long
and every day the riot raged:
hammering, the shovel's scrape,
the shrieking saw through joist
and plaster piercing. Far worse –
what really hurt, got me fretting
were the stereo's pulsating boom,
the deejay's manic yammering;
the yells and curses of builders –
their macho bursts of chorusing...

This morning
I lay late, slept on, got up
in unexpected stillness and –
going outside – found they'd gone,
having left next door a shining skin.
In my front yard they've left a veil
on path and weed, a tell-tale bloom –
a fine white dust on everything. Inside
they've left me my silence;
and in my room, this black sprinkling –
thin words in ink that try to sing...

## Penrhiwceiber Road

Outside the window
your fuchsias flare pink, red
and purple in the afternoon sun.
It's busy out there.
Bumble-bees cling briefly
to bowed heads, then
bob to neighbouring blooms.

Inside this unlit room
where I wait,
it is quiet and cool…

Outside, the 60.A
with a clash of brakes –
a whoosh of air,
squeezes its way through
double-parked cars
in the long terraces.
Bus-pass shoppers
on their stop/go way to Aberdare.

Inside, lazing in a chair,
I start forward at the clack
of the letterbox…

Outside, the postman, in shorts
and trainers, looking sweaty
under his big red, shoulder-strapped-sac
goes padding past the window:
a mailman with a mission –
the clink of the gate records his fast departure.

Cocooned in your quiet room
I sink back to a disconnect
free from toil and time…

Outside, screech of tyres
as a car allows a speeding ambulance through –
blue flashes sweep the ceiling.
Over the road, old Annie
lowers one walking-stick
to tug a weed from her step.

I settle again
into my quiet oasis.
The room grows dim…

Out there the sun has moved
over the roof, drawn a shade
across your fuchsias, but the bees slave on
besotted by the siren flowers…
They have so much to do
and have little time.

Inside it is calm,
a quiet hinterland where
I hardly breathe…

The gate's clink announces
your return. The street door opens
and you enter.
*Hello! I'm back,* you call…
and you bring the busy *outside*
*in.*

## On a Footbridge over the Dare

Mid-May,
purring and chortling away
 under my feet, the Dare runs clear
  but tinted like
  un-milked tea.
   Two weeks of sun have left
    thousands of water polished pebbles high
     and dry leaving the river bank in pleasing slate-
     grey shades – somewhat blemished
     by a single terracotta brick…
   A place of heavy shadows
  for here the Dare has dug its channel
  deep, pushing laurel and ash to
  double their usual heights.
 A sun-searchlight cuts the gloom,
 floods the footbridge with light
and illuminates at eye-level
the rise, jink and fall of
a hundred midges in a dogfight…
 The frantic wing-clap of
  a wood pigeon getting away startles –
  a few small feathers float down…
   Close by, just discernable over
    the water-gossip, the tweeting of
    small birds, and from further
     off the gabble of students released
     from St John's…
   A nearby ash tree stands leafless
   but for a few buds on the airy high twigs.
   Otherwise, luxuriant greenery borders
  the river's course: the abnormal reach
 and spread of laurels, their leather-
thick glossy leaves contrast with the lime-
green pennies of the snowberry thickets…

Heads together,
three schoolgirls thumbing
their mobiles, whispering and giggling
squeeze by...
 Moving to a different time frame
  the Dare, oblivious to transient things, purrs along
  under my feet, forever going and going –
   never gone...

## Embraced

I've come again to the head of the dell,
to the old elm and the ancient boulder.
A fine rain is falling, yet I like this place well –
although why, I can't say. And still the tree holds
the itinerant stone like a caring mother:
for though the tree is old, a low good limb
tight loops the rock as though to press it to her.
The stone has settled in, become a fosterling –
especially as the pair sport matching quilts
of thick mosses, a luxuriant green cover
embellished now with bright, butter yellow coins
the elm's released in this wet October
twilight. An old elm log – at least traces
of it – rots into the earth beside me
swamped in swathes of seeding dog's mercury
that burrs and clings to my coat, clots the laces
of my boots… In heavy earth-scent rising
I am one with the rain, rock and tree. This
is refuge where I stand quiet in a strange bliss…
The only sound the drip, drip of rain falling
from elm leaves over me…

# IV. Obsessions

## Couple

Once,
This house was
A shell with a stone stair
That climbed to a gaping sky and the loud crow;
Now, the **house** is thatched with thick glossy hair
Since holly settled in the **chimney** hollow;
Firm roots have **anchored in** the **flags** below,
Evergreen leaves billow **high** in the air,
Boughs cradle the **walls and beams** that bow
And red berries brighten **the window** square.
**And in dark times** of **stone–shake** and bough-tear
**Under the rain's hammer, the driven snow,**
**the time-worn walls hold firm in the** tree's **care;**
**the house is old, the** tree **young, even so**
They are **so wrapped up in** the **strength they share**
**they should last as long as** their **love affair.**

## Shape-Shifter

Through November's narrow days
not one solitary peep.
In the long murmuring of the rain
not a whisper, no rumour –
nothing of you.

But there was that odd day
when the sun, that old fugitive, smirked
for one brief hour, stirred me
out of torpor and called me to the window
at the exact second
the sleek stranger was passing
down the lane.

On clocking me, she turned, stretched up
and placed her forepaws
on the pane to fix me
with her forthright glare.

Blue-collared, silver-belled:
beauty in chic black fur.

For a full unblinking minute
she held me with her green-glass stare,
regaled me with her purr.
Then she dropped away and vanished.

And though it seems absurd,
when I think back
on what occurred, and on that mogg's departing mew –
there grows a strange conviction:
perhaps the pussycat was you...

## Junk Mail

It got to me
that darkest winter when
it hit the mat – mail catalogue
of comfort styles
from *Nightingales*

They got to me
those zesty springtime sales
the summer chic from *Nightingales*
the right name
wrong address

It gets to me
at the letterbox's clack
autumn's new colours glossed in cellophane
neatly wrapped
addressed to you

It still gets to me
this fashionable mockery –
unkind gag sent by a cruel intercessor
but I know it isn't so –
just an un-redirected mag'

Yes it still gets to me
a book of dresses tops and gloves
a last tenuous linking that's destined to stop
and when it does
will it get to me?

## Rapunzel

Midnight, and I am here, heart-a-drum
under your high tower, for down
over the stones of your keep you have trailed
and let fall the dark Niagara of your hair.
Now, a soft sigh, perhaps from the high
sill where spills your glimmering braids.
But no, it is only me dreaming,
or the tongues of trees that murmur
to the night wind. There is nothing,
no glinting hair, no call from the tower –
the impossible wall – no face
at the dark casement; no one there.
The lustre, the lovely gloss, is just frost
on ivy under the moon's white stare.

## Disclosure (Felled Pine. 2014)

*For Rebecca*

You lived long, unregarded, when you stood
with kin, but now, sap-drained and out of breath
you manifest yourself stretched out in death
blocking the way that runs off through the wood.
I touch your outer circle and find from
backward counting that you were just a seed
when youthful blood was drained in streams to feed
a future blaze of flowers on the Somme.
And here, hand's length from when you were a pine
of single bud – I came to be. But fate
as you well know is wayward, for at this line
within a heart's width of your bark came she:
fair, slender slip ( fifty rings too late )
– to sow all heaven and a hell in me.

## When You Enter

the endless desert of the dispossessed
you'll walk a grey world: ever and always
before you the dull dunes. No view to arrest
the eye, sameness, where nothing will amaze:
no calling oasis, no breathtaking crest.
Aimless, arbitrary, are the turns you'll take,
for no track appears that offers a quest —
nothing to aim for to relieve the ache
of a lost heartland. Now, you are the guest
of an everywhere uniformity
that runs on forever north, east, south
and west. There will be no welcoming house,
no lovely face; but you will be free
of desire, by no fickle passion possessed.

# V. Dark Side

## The Predator

Was it fear that woke me into the half light –
broke me from the dream of wildebeest,
from the snorts, the white-eyed streaming-thunder
of a great migration?

I lie in the covers, listening.
Far off on the expressway, the faint roar of
the 7.00 am rush – from which
I'm now excluded.

I had sensed that he was close –
the dark lion – his great yellow eyes
on stragglers (a weak one) glare fixed
in a chilling focus, rising
for the take.

And there, close-by, a footfall,
and now a purr, low, – but loud enough to waken:
the dairyman and his gliding float.
Eyes closed I hold a picture –
the fresh putting out, the empties taken.

## Hill Farm

Billy is down to chewing
gorse, holly-bark and dock.
Mown hay in lower plot
is sunk in muck and ruined.
The wood-pile's low and soaked –
the heap of ash is higher –
last heartwood of the oak
spits out more smoke than fire.
The sky has spread a shawl
that's darkened field and hill;
sharp showers whip and trawl,
the house groans at the shrill
east-gusts of blurring weight
that hit the stack, steal the slate...

The rain comes harsh again,
it's flooded-out the yard
and drowned the speckled hen.
It's never rained so hard.
No reason now to stay –
the mantel clock has stopped
and time has run away.
The path into the cwm
has grown so dark – but not
as dark as inner gloom.
The rain won't stop. It just
remains to close the door,
free Billy from his post,
pat his puzzled head, and go...

## Mopping Up

The green seclusion of the alder wood
shattered by the shouts of boys; and the thud
of a stone – and fleeing from a blitz of rocks,
suddenly before me a flushed-out fox.
A lurching revenant, half-furred and thin
dragging a rear leg chewed to a red stick
by the bite and bind of an iron gin –
the other hind-limb, a gangrenous stump.
We face each other, the dog-fox and I:
the dying, not-yet-dying, eye to eye,
till the cudgel carrying boys burst in
upon our little space – and he tries to swing
aside to get away; but he is ill and stiff
and the saving whack from my walking staff
breaks the remaining vestige of his will.
Fist on his scruff, I lug him to a clear rill,
plunge him in and hold him down (with youths
now silent, standing round) and see, through
ice-cold flowing glass, his fading glare;
his lolling tongue; his hanging jaw – where
tiny silver bubbles lift-off, one by one,
and then they cease… and it is done…

## Tracks in the Snow

All day I slogged through a deep silence of snow,
strayed through a whiteness, empty, unoccupied;
so I was cheered when a sheep-path showed,
when far in the locked land a curlew cried.
Life-signs, in spite of the drifts that smothered:
script of rabbit across a hill, and beyond –
the tracks of ponies; many bird prints covered
snow-skim on the ice-decking of a pond.
Then, in blinding-white, a boot-print braille,
and on some whim – a pattern repeating –
I, treading so softly, followed the trail
that a fresh fall of snow was fast deleting;
and found him, he, whose white untenanted eye
mirrored a blank oblivious sky...

## The President
*(for A.E.)*

Because only you knew
how close he was, how quickly he was gaining,
you cooked up a covert strategy
to get your girl away – away to a retreat
across the border.

And so the race began:
armed with attaché case and mobile
you issued dispatches
chased replies, sent and received
uncountable texts.
You marshalled friends and allies.

Employing defensive tactics
you sandbagged harassed positions
with pillows and cushions.
You diverted the enemy
with bursts of radio;
received aid in capsules
and survived on air rations
from cylinders.

For twelve long months
hardly bearable the blows
you suffered – yet never moaned,
but hung on… hung on… until
you gained the neutral ground,
re-grouped, and gifted
your girl another life, a new beginning.

What covert courage.
What last ditch, death defying brinkmanship,
for having got her there – within a day –
you gave the game away
by dying…

## Penrhiwceiber Colliery
### 1872 – 1985

Men conceived me as slave, built me out of steel
and brick, but I've outgrown them – now I control.
They come to me and grovel – that's the deal.
Their reward? – to suck dust for a scratch of coal.
I am Reformer: I ink the Cynon black
as Acheron and sludge Ceiber's green meadows.
Benefactor too: I make tired wives widows.
I grant men a gasp of rest, then haul them back:
at my compelling blasts, my wolfhound hoots,
drum wheels roll, teeth mesh and ropes vibrate
and with a clattering of hobnail boots
the blackened companies I regurgitate.
More men, pale as moths, I drop into the deep.
Grimed and beat, I wind them up – some I keep.

*Penrhiwceiber Colliery fell silent in 1985 after
operating for more than a hundred years –
these fourteen lines might have been the
boast hooted out by the pit in its heyday.*

# Ghost Town

I was never a stay-at-home – always
wandering off: gone no more than a day
or so and never more than a mile.
Yet they left, they could have waited awhile.

It was springtime when they abandoned me.
Those who had cars were the first to flee,
then in packed buses others took to the road
followed by lines of lorries with heavy loads.

Within days the town became a dead zone
of empty avenues that I strayed alone,
frowned upon by concrete apartment blocks
where street-level doors were left unlocked –

so I had plenty of food through that summer;
when thirsty I made my way to the river
where I saw flocks of birds and friendly goats
feeding on bank-side grasses and wild oats.

Autumn – water turned bad, food hard to find;
and though weeds heaved up asphalt and climbed
the walls, the well fed goats lay down and died.
Hundreds of starlings fell out of the sky.

Hooded men clad in green plastic appeared,
and one, bread in hand tried to lure me near,
but I limped away, recognizing a trick:
in his other hand was a gun that clicked.

Not that I could manage food anymore –
my throat was a furnace, swollen, raw.
All dogs have their day, well that's how I felt
with my paws peeling and losing my pelt.

When winter arrived, from its chill I hid
in a hole under a concrete pyramid.
In that place was a glow that dispelled night –
a crack in the wall gave a warm blue light…

**Witness**

Selma watched little puffs of cotton-wool clouds
drifting across endless blue above
the slow glide of the East River.

There was still quite a heap of urgent mail
waiting to be cleared from her desk, but this was
her winding-down-day, her last day.

Tomorrow, she and her love-buddy, Hank,
were escaping – flying to a three week break
in Santa Barbara.

She kept glancing at her watch, only 08.41.
Time was dragging. She needed her vacation, and although
the day outside was lovely, Selma was wishing it away.

The distant, tall Chrysler building began to quiver
in the warming air, and through the open vent
along the base of the plate glass

the hum and hoot of traffic on Broadway, 80 floors
below, was just discernable. Selma checked
her watch again and sighed, 08.45.

She looked north towards the sister tower –
squinty-eyed from the easterly glare –
and saw with some surprise
the sun glance off a falling silver arrow…

# Trans-Dark

Maybe it's when
from a kiss and *Take care,*
you return to your house at the path's end;
but the end is dark, and there's nothing there...

And maybe then,
defeated, lost in a storm,
you fall upon barefoot prints in snow
of an unseen child who might shepherd you home.

It might be when
caught in a cold moon,
clawed by twig and bark in an owl-haunted wood,
you shiver awake in quilted feathers, in your own dark room.

Or it's when
as you gulp and smother,
and see, deep in swaying veils of kelp –
floating hair, and a face with the eyes of your mother.

Maybe it's when
quiet and stretched in
chilly equanimity, you enter the warming
glow of a rose – at seventeen hundred or so degrees...

And maybe then
you'll take a lane of strange allure,
that you somehow know will end before
a familiar house – that welcomes you with an open door.

# VI. Speleo

## Ogof Fawr

                    Yes, this is how
it was. Sneaking away on his own –
he just had to know, had to descend
through the drizzle of a long-ago-December dusk,
down into that ancient depression, to the base
of the broken face and the dark mouth
that gulped the fast stream,
run-off from miles of misted forest – miles
of shrouded moor.
                    Did I know him
that reckless youth? Who all those years ago
stood before the dark gape in that forlorn
far off place, steadying heart, summoning nerve.
I think that he ducked quickly through the
raft of froth, the peat-brown, thigh-deep water
at the threshold; then over shattered rock-teeth
of the lower jaw – and a into chilling
spray-swept darkness.
                    Perhaps I recall
that he threw the coiled rope ahead, into the black
throat, then stepped tentatively forward – and out
onto the nightmare ramps of Ogof Fawr.
And that's all it took, the small pressure of
his step – and the trap closed...
                    The floor falling –
    the terrible thunder.
And before his light failed
I think he saw –
in the blurring vibration,
    the blocks – coffin sized – detaching
        from the dripping walls.
            Yes, that's how it was:
                    tons of water,
                tons of rock – avalanching
        in a strange,
                    unstoppable slow motion
                            into a black abyss.

                    I was aware of something
odd about his right foot, a strange stickiness
between his fingers, the foetid stink of crushed rock on
the rushing air.  I'm near certain there was no
quick replay of a past life,
                    only the deafening fast-
                              slow-
                                        fall

                              and the calm though:
                                                  *What now?*
          A heavy blow to his head –

then nothing...

               Perhaps I recall that
he was prey, discarded to one side of falling thunder
that reverberated on and on. I think I saw him lying –
prising apart fingers glued together by blood, feeling
for, finding the helmet (split open like a gaping shell,)
the smashed lamp.
               Do I remember
his agonising exodus? I'm not certain. Black cascading
water, darkness. The sting of lacerated arms, burning
head. And did he limp like a beaten dog: dragging an
outsize foot across miles of sucking moor, through
miles of dripping fir-forest?
Who was he?  I no longer know.
               Long ago along with
slivers of glass, a twisting of rope, deep in the midnight
of Ogof Fawr, maybe some fragments of bone were
interred.  Perhaps he never left...

               Yet, under the sun,
when I wander too far the blistering roads of summer
my right heel aches to the bone – too sore to set my weight
upon – and I have to turn,
and limp for home...

74

## Pant Mawr Moor (2013)

*A digger takes a tea-break*

You ascend scaffolding into a lesser dark –
into a January hailstorm.
And although your canvas suit's coated
with a ten pound handicap of not-so-glorious mud
you execute a fast dash for cover, drop
to your knees, squeeze under a slanted, corrugated sheet
weighted down against the low ruin of a wall.
You're hot, sweat-soaked –
but not for long. And you think:
*What the hell am I doing here?*

You hunker down in your little bolt-hole
and there, in the one remaining corner
of an ancient sheepfold,
take your thirty minute break.
The nails of a night demon rasp and rattle
on the iron sheet. Hail – snowberry sized – jets through
gaps and chinks in the ruined wall.
You reach for your flask and think:
*This is crazy. What am I doing here?*

Teeth chattering you cower under clattering steel,
only your palms, cradling the thermos-cup, warm.
You squint out into the night where your helmet beam gives
back iced barrenness beneath a louring sky.
The great moor, contemptuous of man's handy-work
reclaims its stones, has levelled the hill-farmers house and barn.
Across the high plateau – unopposed –
the skirmishing easterly finds you;
converts your sweaty under-suit to an icy wrap.

As you shiver uncontrollably, there's a lull
in the wind's howl, and high in the night and stretching away
you catch the far thunder of a big liner: fun-people escaping,
flying to hot sun, warm sand,
while you are ten miserable miles from wheels –
from anywhere – and you think:
*What in God's name am I doing here?*

Pant Mawr takes back its stones,
Farm and byre gone,  foundations, razed.
Lichens, mosses – green and mustard hued – spread
a smothering shroud. A few tottering blocks stand
as memorial to generations of men's toil –
pale straws, remnants of last year's nettles,
their bouquet of remembrance.
And you ask yourself: *What **am** I doing here?*

Then you think of your mates,
two hundred feet below the moor, sweating, cursing,
and with sinew and steel, forcing
a thin superficial vein.
Dreaming of finding and following some great vena cava
that forever snakes to the portals and atriums
of the moor's deep heart,
to the enduring chambers of stone.

## Mynydd Cilsanws

*(for Toby Stewart 1971 – 2004 . Caver)*

Fifth day of July, the evening cool
now that this first decent rain
in weeks has broken
the long, hot hold of June.
Like you, so many times before
I've taken the rising path that twists
through dense bracken on the hill's west side –
ancient Cilsanws has lost its head
in a fine white mist.

Ferns hiss softly in the fresh breeze, shift and sway.
At my every step on the narrow path
I'm brushed by frond, blocked by stem – held
to the only way allowed through
a waving, green ocean.
A stonechat flits from fern-tip to
fern-tip…

Chak! chak! twee! – such a big commotion
from a little bird; then I see why: he's courting
*two* females. What makes him irresistible?
Is it his orange chest or his dark brown cap
and white collar? Chak! chak! twee!
with every call his stub tail flicks up
and down.

Here, the sea of bracken breaks, gives
onto a rough island of grit and heather. I rest
on the big flat slab – a thing you never did.
The recent rain has summoned up battalions
of glistening black slugs, in deliberate
slimy slow-motion, they slide the succulent green,
browse purple ling and the sweet wild strawberry.

And now at last, the pathless place
of tumbled rock, where, under the skylark's song,
only fern and foxglove flourish; and here, remote
and unvisited in the grit-block chaos –
the box-like pit of sheer-sided stone.

This, your place of lonely pilgrimage –
this square of missing ground.
Here, under the drumming sun and the hail's lash
you heaved and hauled the only way
that you knew how: recklessly down
and deeper
down,
risking all.

No mark remains of your impassioned toil.
Time has tanned your tumbled stones
to a dark grey conformity. Except
that in a corner, shadowed
by the foxgloves' chime-less spires,
a tiny portal: a rusted iron door
that you alone have dared.

For against all odds, you found
that dark forsaken land. Others,
a few, have raised that creaking vent,
glimpsed the dark descending stair,
but lacked the nerve to enter.

Light fades, rain clouds threaten.
I take the short way home, out
across the Darren's high ledges.
Paired ravens lift, wheel in wide circles
and scold me on my way.
Their hollow croaks seem inconsiderately loud
in the airy silence.
Brief is the thought they might wake you...

## Breakthrough

Madman with a hazel switch I swat about
my head – there are devils in this Eden
that I dread: dancing marsh mosquitoes
and legions of the midge that drift the air
like motes of snow. I don't know which is worse
the torment here above or the terror
down below.

It has always been – this crater
covened by the trees; it was here
before the oak was named, before the ice
withdrew, before it came. Green hollow
gouged in Gower's side, mysterious,
holding its secret from age to age till
Taylor and his sisters read the signs –
saw the serpent rise, heaving from its hollow
white with rage.

Six months hard toil, some moments of terror, but now
key blocks have shifted, a door has opened and
I've jammed a foot in the gap. Twisting to view down
beyond my boot, I glimpse the maker – the black silk
of its sleeping surface. Fifty years ago
that little terrier, Maurice Taylor
went one better...

Here, while his two sisters fretted high above,
he gulped a big breath, held it, then surrendering –
slipped down, neck-deep and gasping, into
an icy grip to gaze into a great darkness.
I'm no terrier with a lion's heart, but
I bring a dull green dough; tiny silvered cylinders;
bright coloured threads: yellow, black, blue and red –
elements of a potent spell.

I place the spell. Make a careful upward retreat,
an extrication from night, from silence, up
through a nest of sweating boulders – tight tensed –
on up through the twilight zone where
a nameless digger has left his stressed and rusting steel –
the amount of metal a measure of his fear. Up, and
out into the gloomy-green of Tree Cavern – to
birdsong and the flies' drone.

I take deep breaths – stretch tall – under a roof
high raftered with ash and hazel, released from
the rock's dark press. Lady-fern removes cold clay
from my palms and I kneel for the spell's casting.
Yellow is applied with thumb and finger, then
red to the opposing pole – instantly a muffled thud –
and a smoke-wraith rising…

A feet first slither back to darkness, deep through
a chaos of blocks cradled in six months of creaking iron –
down, down to the deep end. Maurice, Marjorie, Eileen –
you too, unknown digger of the dark, be with me now
in spirit: the hill is breached, the way is wide, the keeper
sleeps beside the door, and down the silent canyons
the lakes of midnight stretch before.

## Persephone

I have lain here forever
under bunching contours
where the road climbs steep
on Craig Y Castell.
All day they pass, travellers,
eyes only for the road –
minds on distant destinations.

Some stop awhile to look
upon the land below –
every level place and easy slope branded,
bearing the signature of their own kind.
Farmsteads thin sown
on green patchwork shawls.
Fields held by neat walls, pleached hedges.
Narrow lanes stringing
farms, byres and barns.

In the quick flicker of a century, a few –
fewer than the fingers on a hand – stop,
stand long, sensing a mystery:
sensing me.
They gaze, as lovers might, upward
over the bleak rugged back of Cefn Onnau
where man has left no mark,
where only ragged sheep have hoofed
their thin scribbles.

At my beckoning, they will climb
with downcast gaze,
stepping – as in a dream,
the tawny hide of Cefn Onnau,
knee-deep through the drag of brown bracken
rough-brushed east by winter winds.
Above my head they will scour the grey
arroyos of stone, probe the pits

and gullies of ephemeral streams seeking
a high reaching fibrilla – a thread
of my dark and rising hair.

They, or their progeny, will seek me out
again and again. Root long in the pelt
of moss and rush, the dour ruck
of block and boulder that conceals me.
Thwarted, they may be distracted by
the brightness of the sparse berries
that glint from the gloom of
the lonely holly, but I am not there.
Nor there in the dark crevice
under the shadow of the crabbed thorn.
And they will halt and shiver when
they think they hear my sighing,
but it is only the mountain wind caressing
the rock hollow
that makes the sheltering harts-tongue quiver.

But one of these, one of the few,
will find the single stone –
one insignificant stone that conceals
the far-flung filament of my darkness,
and he will raise the stone,
thrill at my cool breath,
breathe a purer air.

I am deathless:
dark and lovely, cold and cruel as Ayesha;
yet this one I will seduce away,
even from the bluest summer sky; the sun's kiss.
In fear and amazement
he will come to me...

## The Discoverer

He was always there. Something about the gorge
and the grey rock drew him as if he'd mislaid
a treasure there. Month after month he laid siege
to the slopes, leaving scars: boulders dislodged
and tumbled, disturbed ground. Then one day

high up in a steep gully, as he slipped
over slabs – the slicked winter-stones, probing
every shadow, undercut and crevice,
he found something low in a rock-face: a fist-
sized mouth that whispered of a world within.

He laboured to split the gully stream, rigged
a good water-ribbon to the dark throat.
The thirsty mouth guzzled, gulped and swigged,
so he offered the rich fluorescent slug –
it took that too, did not back up or choke.

Descending the mountain, he leaned on a beech
bough over the deep run of the river.
Wrapped close in his coat, he waited, watched
the clear current undulate and pitch
about its blocks. He dozed. Woke, – with a shiver

to the hiss and slide of a green snake. He splashed
upstream to a tight fissure where the loud stain
oozed back to day. He set a fire in the niche,
witnessed the niche's lust for smoke and ash,
and his mind was fired by the swallowed flame.

Back at the top of the gully, white smoke
flagged above an ivy covered scar.
He tore away branch, root and boulder, broke
through to a strange new world. He looked, poked
and pried till that world paled, became familiar.

Then he left, intending to return to what
was found – to the thing known, but he never did.
Sometimes, he thought perhaps he should have quit
when he awoke in wonder as a green snake slicked
by, or when he burned for what the ivy hid.

# VII. Other

## Under Gunnera

The hot sun everywhere –
around and in her.
Raising her dress, she toed off
first her left, then her right sneaker and
entered the water-mirror.
Breath bated, slowly she waded
a pool, deep and secretive.
Oh, and how the sun flashed
from the nudged surface,
how caressing the cool liquid
that lacquered and lapped
her bare legs. The shore closer now, where
a dipper waded and dived; where
wagtails splashed and curtseyed.

Out of the water, a hobble up
a clatter of hot pebbles, and
she'd made it: achieved
a thing long desired, arrived
where she'd always dreamed of being –
*Cabbage Island.*
How huge and strange the jungle
of luxuriant green umbrellas.
How beautiful the damsels' shimmer
the whirring flicker and drone of dragonflies,
the iridescent blues and jades
of a thousand sunbathers:
the dazed beetles and bugs heat-spread
and still on the emerald plage.

Stooping, she slipped under and in, was
taken and wrapped by a cool green twilight.
She passed between ribbed stems
fat as cucumbers, that pillared high over her head
to the green chalices that
sapped the solar swelter.

In wonder, she wandered wide and far
a mysterious green marquee,
whose temperate air, form and order seemed
to hint at some unseen guardian-keeper.
Finding a pretty arbour, she spread herself
out in a green pleasure: pillowed on her sneakers,
a shingle mattress for her bed.

An abrupt darkening; a flash; then
a clap of thunder; a brief, but heavy pattering
on the cupped umbrellas – and
every drop promptly rendered from roof to
root by the fluted risers, so that
not a drip nor droplet found her.
Risen between pebbles at her feet,
turgid and spear-capped, a young upright shoot;
for all the world as though to
stem any rain-tear in the taut membrane.
Dazed by the high-low, razor-buzz
of a bluebottle, drowsed
by the closeness of the green air, she sank
into deep green sleep, and a dream…

…where, in a surging odour of river water,
into her bedchamber came
an eager suitor
that stretched over her.
And then, something akin to pain –
but not pain, persistent, repeated and
repeated that almost broke her
from her green rapture.

It wasn't the mutter of thunder with-
drawing, nor the chilling of air with the sun's
falling. It came far across water-meadow and wood:
the crying out of a girl's name that rang and
rang from a mother's tongue –
a frantic calling . . . calling . . .

## The Red Shop

There is a place
where six roads meet, there, brazen
on a corner at the very centre of a snare
of streets, stands the Red Shop.
And sometimes in my ceaseless searching
I'd passed that place before, and never thought to stop.
But, on dust-dry streets, on a burning day
in dying June, I was wearied by my quest.
The stare of the sun at noon
had set my goal beyond all grasp – unreachable
the dream I travelled to. Dead beat, I stopped to rest
and found I stood before a half recalled retreat –
the wide, and ever open door of the Red Shop.

Strange déjà vu.
The cool, inviting gloom within
called to me and thrilled me through,
and so – I entered in. Having left the sun's bright glare
I was blind at first, to the forms
of things within the dimness there.
Cool, silent, scented was the gloom,
but in a while, I could perceive that other
travellers languished in shadowed corners
of the shuttered room. Some stood alert,
others lay fatigued, all faced one way –
wide-eyed – with an adoring gaze towards
a curtained inner door, a deeper shade
wherein a striking figure stood.
So fair the form, so still the shape,
awhile I thought that it could only be
some sort of doll – a wondrous mannequin.

Oh how I longed
to look upon the face beyond the shadow
of the drape, and then the doll – it spoke
to me, inside my head seductively:
*Come in! Come in!* And in a deepening daze
I moved to meet the fragrant one,
to stroke the hair, to touch the cheek.
The lily lids were lashed down tight.
The thing – was it succubus or seraphim?
I raised a hand to feel the skin, and then
two sea-green eyes unlashed, two wrecker lights flashed out
and locked on me – oh God the chuckling –
the knowing grin that drew me irresistibly;
it called me on, pulled me in, upon the cherub lips
that sulked with sin, and there I clung
drinking, drinking, in a green and scented ocean
sinking. Round and round, ah the dream I swirled
around in, down, and down – spellbound –
in a fragrant heaven drowning, drowning.

Thus I drank from lips divine,
fed upon a flesh exalted, and never dreamed
how cruelly the feast was salted;
for in that cool place, on that burning day
a fallen angel quenched my thirst
but took my soul away. Now,
the centre of my world is the Red Shop.
No longer aimless is my questing, through dusk
or dark, or bright of day – there I must go
for all the roads of longing lead me there,
and never, never will I know a quiet spot  to rest in
for all the roads away –  are to despair.

## The Crow King

Bede was tired, forlorn. The light was fading,
and still, the marsh – stretching wide to his right –
held him to the wall: a high barrier
of random stone that paralleled his slowing stride;
on it ran, endlessly for mile on mile, and out of sight
without break, breech, gate or stile.

A sudden high-piping call, the frantic wing-clap
of some unknown bird, beyond the wall –
stopped Bede in his tracks.
Enough. He'd had enough of endless wall.
Right there and then he raised a boot,
both arms, to probe, to palm the stones
for gap and chink wide enough to offer
grip for fingertip and toe.

Not easy, for although the wall stood
two-man high, it stood in good repair.
He persevered, toe and hand, until, thief-like –
Bede heaved his head above
the capping-stones to spy the land beyond.
It wasn't what he saw there
so much as what he smelt,
that so disconcerted and appalled him:
a sickening, all pervading odour
of putrefying flesh.

As for the view: bland –
an inclined plane lifting to the far off summit
of a grey moor; a rhiw of tall rush
and tussock-grass stretching left into the darkness
of the east, and right to the darkening west.
Hoisting a leg, Bede straddled the wall,
scraping a shin; he followed
with the other leg, then sliding over,
dropped in;

down, into a buzzing,
angry drone; a rising wail of blue-black radiation.
Everywhere – stashed
in the luxuriant, suffocating rush – fetid flesh;
slimed fur; hair and bone of the flies feast.
Bede held his breath,
dashed on and up, deeper into
the clutching grass and rush, then
stopped short –
startled, suddenly afraid –
for almost right away, he was confronted
by a scarecrow.

Dwarf-like – not conspicuously tall
as scarecrows should be –
it had no legs. Its hat, just
topping the tips of the tallest rush.
From its shoulders sagged
a ragged lichened coat. An elm stick
crutched an outstretched arm, the stick-hand open,
palm forward, as though to bar Bede's way.
And on the grotesque face, an expression
that seemed to shout. **Who are you?**
**This place is mine. Get out.**

Three paces separated them. It glared
at Bede. He stared back: wide-eyed,
unbreathing, hypnotised by
the cold, white-china eyes
sunk in the crumpled canvas face.
In all that dense, luxuriant sea,
that bleak, extended sprawl,
by what coincidence, or fate,
should the thing *be there* at all? *Right there*
as if to face Bede, to intercept him
at the very place he scaled the wall.

Behind the dwarf's shoulder,
rising-moon glow, a dark flight of torn-cloud,
and from the east, a chill wind
that set the rush-spikes swaying.
Bede broke from the thing's gaze –
its level glare, began again,
to breath; and looking around, thought –
*Why here? A scarecrow here*
*on ground that held no crop –*
*no sign of barley, oats or rye for him to guard,*
*no fruiting bush, or tree within ten miles,*
*and with spring long gone –*
*not one new lamb to offer up a tender eye.*

Bede's head turned, as if against his will,
until again he faced the gargoyle gaze,
the mouth like a dark cave. **Get out.**
it seemed to say. **Get off trespasser.**
**Get out. Here, you have no right-of-way.**

**Pruk. Pruk.** A hoarse, **Pruk. Pruk.**
From the dark ground, heavy wing flap,
and – as if conjured from nowhere, by
a slick magician's trick –
up hopped a great raven
that hooked upon the thing's wrist
and with deep croaks and clicks,
it settled, perched there,
bold as bold could be, and fixed
its black-bead eyes on Bede.

Hard and chill blew the east wind,
launching a moon full-sail in the streaming clouds.
And all around, from the thrash and heave
of the ground, rose the raucous caws
of rooks, the guttural squawks of crows.
Up flapped a jackdaw, alighted
on the scarecrow's shoulder – so
rook and raven were familiars of the thing,
and, was it a trick of moonlight – for now
the dwarf seemed to be grinning,
a dark red ichor draining down its jaw – grinning
and growing, its moon-shadow flowing out to enfold Bede.

Bede broke away, fled in terror
over ground thick with death, alive with birds.
Tripping over stripped bone, falling –
face down, hands into putrefaction. Up, up again,
and away he fled through the dark wind;
deep through an inclined ocean of crashing rush; away,
towards the last faint afterglow of western light; away
pursued by the caws of rooks,
the croaks of ravens, by the echoing metallic laughter
of the daws, and the monstrous shadow of the Crow King.
And running with Bede, the wall,
penning him in; the wall,
that so late before had kept him out;
ever on it ran, on and on, unrelenting, without end....